HEAVENLY HOMOS, ETC

Queer Icons from LGBTQ Life, Religion and History

John: Will you look at that? **Tony:** You see it as well?

i

Apocryphile Press
PO Box 255
Hannacroix, NY 12087
www.apocryphilepress.com

Jan Haen gratefully acknowledges that he was inspired by the artwork of Keith Haring, Robert Lentz and Andrew Freshour. Enquiries may be addressed to the artist at jan.haen@kpnmail.nl

Please join our mailing list at
www.apocryphilepress.com/free
We'll keep you up to date on all our new releases,
and we'll also send you a FREE BOOK. Visit us today!

CONTENTS

Introduction	iv	Alan Turing	54
		Harvey Milk	58
Heavenly Homos	1	George Duncan	62
Sebastian	2	Matthew Shepard	66
The Bible	7	Mychal Judge	71
David and Jonathan	9	Fanny Ann Eddy	75
Lesbianism, Procreation and Masturbation	11	Mary Daly	79
Sodom and Gomorrah	14	David Kato	83
Ruth and Naomi	17	Xulhaz Mannan and Mahbub Rabbi Tonoy	87
The Beloved Disciple	20	Bisexuality	91
Sergius and Bacchus	28	Virginia Woolf	92
Brigid and Darlughdach	32	Pansexuality and Asexuality	96
Hildegard von Bingen	35	
Aelred of Rievaulx	38	Jan van Kilsdonk	99
Joan of Arc	42	Danell Leyva	102
Transgender	47	
Walatta Petros	48	Sources	103
Juana Ines de la Cruz	51		

INTRODUCTION

Most people expect that a newborn baby
will consciously or unconsciously turn out
to be heterosexual.

But there are some babies who at some point
or other in their lives discover or become aware
that they are homosexual, lesbian, bisexual,
transgender, or even asexual.

In this graphic book, you will find brief sketches
of persons who—rightly or wrongly—were
presumed to be homosexual, lesbian, bisexual,
transgender, or asexual.

I believe that heteros and homos etc. long
to be respected and loved in equal measure.

This is my motivation for the making of this book.

—Jan Haen

Tony: "Heavenly homos"—where did that come from?

John: Well, today (November 2) Catholics celebrate *All Souls' Day* and yesterday they celebrated *All Saints'*.

Tony: Yes, I remember a story about Pope John XXIII. He was asked whether he believed "Hell" existed. He answered, "Yes, but I don't think there is anybody to be found in it."

John: Right! So let us look at some gay icons no longer living.

Tony: The big favorite is without a doubt **SAINT SEBASTIAN**.

He was born in Narbonne, France in 256 AD and died in 288.

He converted to Christianity and was baptized secretly because Christians were persecuted at that time, and he was a Roman soldier.

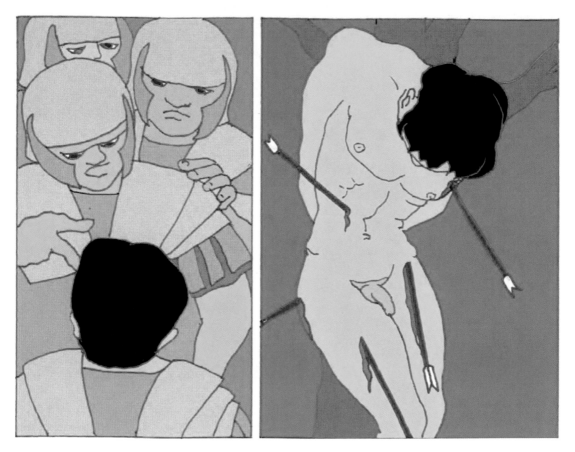

During the reign of Diocletian, fellow soldiers discovered that Sebastian was a secret Christian. He was arrested, tied naked to a tree, shot with arrows, and left for dead.

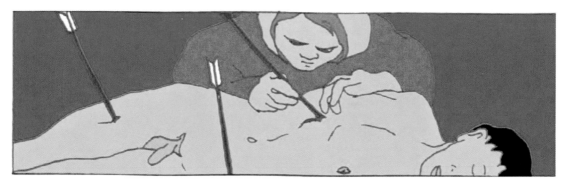

Irene, the widow of Castulus, wanted to bury him, but discovered that he was still alive. She took him home and nursed him back to health.

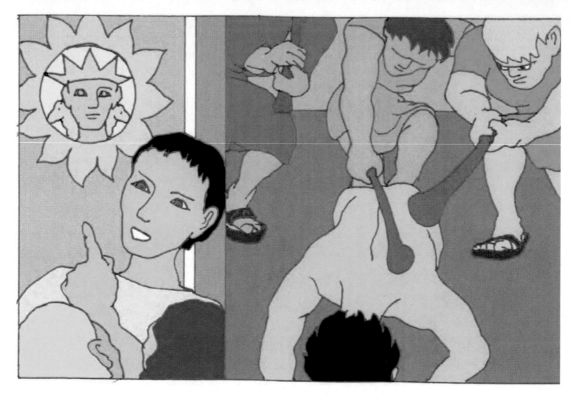

A few days later Sebastian stood on the steps of Sol Invictus Temple (the unconquered sun god, patron of soldiers). He accused the emperor of injustice towards Christians. Again, he was arrested, stripped and beaten to death in the Circus of Rome.

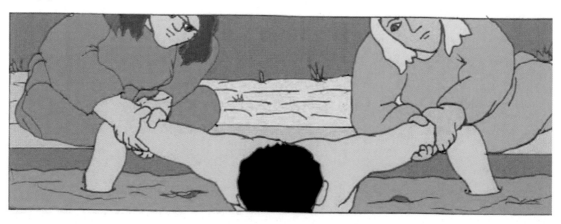

His body was dumped in the Cloaca Maxima, the Roman sewer. Irene and/or Lucinda recovered his body, cleaned it and buried him in the catacomb along the Via Appia.

The Basilica of St. Sebastian-Outside-the-Walls was originally built in the first half of the 4th century and his remains were placed there around 350 AD. The present edifice is a largely 17th century construction. St. Sebastian is remembered with a sculpture under an altar as shown here.

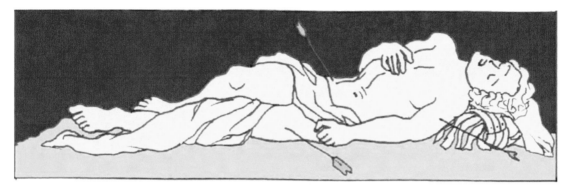

Sebastian was proclaimed patron saint of archers, soldiers, gardeners, tailors, plague victims, and fire brigades. Many churches throughout the world have depictions of St. Sebastian in some form or other.

Traditional   Modern   Provocative

Tony: But was he gay?

John: We don't know. But it seems to have everything to do with the sheer sensuality of his portrayals. See here the way Peter Paul Rubens depicted him early in the 17th century......

And then there is also the fact that gays can identify with the suffering of Sebastian and his sense of betrayal.

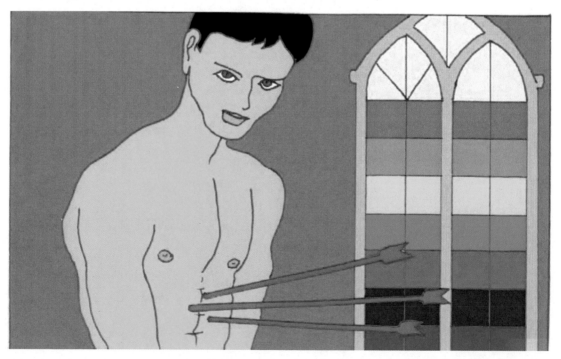

Tony: Where did all this negativity come from?

John: In the Bible, in the Book of Leviticus (Old Testament), it is written: *"You must not lie with a man as with a woman. This is a hateful thing"* (Lev. 18:22). *"The man who lies with a man in the same way as with a woman: they have done a hateful thing together; they must die; their blood be on their heads"* (Lev. 20:13).

7

John: This biblical condemnation of homosexual activity determined the persecution of homos throughout the centuries. Even today, anti-gays base their biases, prejudices, and anti-homo activities on these Biblical passages.

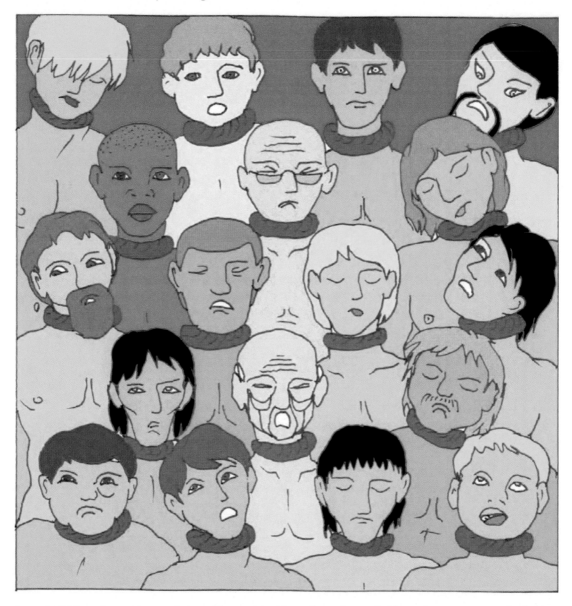

In 1731, in Utrecht, the Netherlands, following complaints, eighteen "sodomites" (men having sex with men) were arrested and condemned to death by strangling.

John: Yet for all that, it is claimed that **JONATHAN**, the son of King Saul, fell in love with **DAVID**, who succeeded Saul as king.

1 Samuel 18:1: *Jonathan's soul became closely bound to David's and Jonathan came to love him as his own soul.*

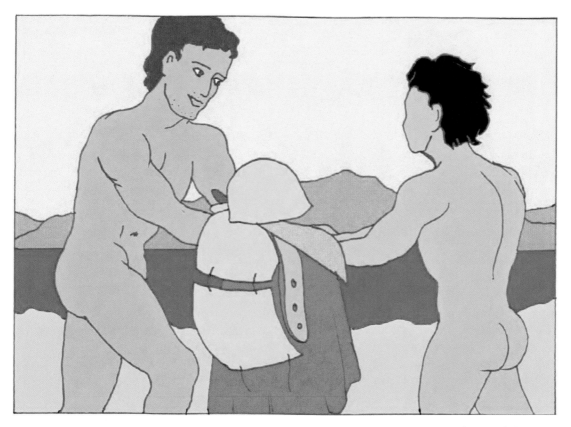

1 Sam. 18:3-4: *Jonathan made a pact with David to love him as his own soul: he took off the cloak he was wearing and gave it to David, and his armor too, even his sword, his bow and his belt.*

John: And then there was David's lament over the death of Jonathan...

"O Jonathan, in your death I am stricken...very dear to me you were; your love to me, more wonderful than the love of a woman" (2 Sam. 1:26).

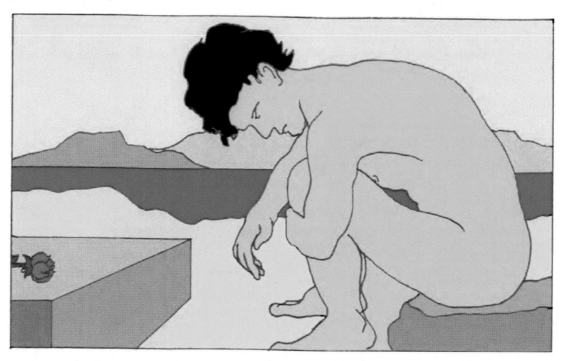

John: The thing is, both Jonathan and David were married. We also know that David's escapades were not exclusively male-oriented.

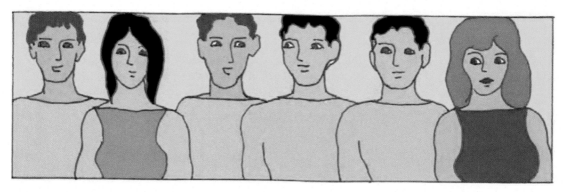

Tony: So was Jonathan gay? Or were they both bisexual?

John: We just don't know.

Tony: We mustn't forget the women.

John: Yes, well there is no specific condemnation for "a woman who lies with a woman, as she does with a man" in the Bible.

Tony: Why?

John: According to the creation story, "Man and woman were created in the image and likeness of God. God blessed them, saying, "Be fruitful, multiply and fill the earth and conquer it" (Gen. 1:27-28).

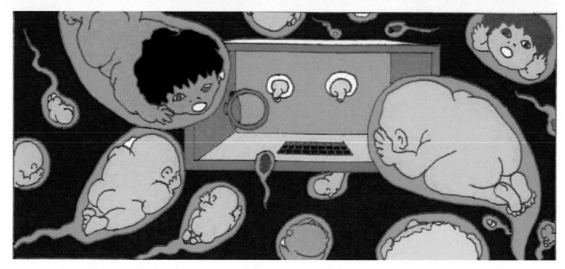

...But it was believed that semen contained in complete form a boy/ girl. When a man sexually impregnated a woman, it meant that the woman served as a sort of "incubator." Only in the "incubator" could the seed boy/girl survive and grow, until the boy/girl was ready to be launched into the world at birth.

...New life, whether male or female, had its origin in the man—not the woman. The woman merely facilitated the process, but had nothing to do with creating new life.

...Which is why the "spilling" of seed, *sperma*, outside of a woman is totally taboo, because the new life contained in the sperma would die. Take the story of Onan, the second son of Judah. He was told to take Tamar to produce a child for his brother, who had died. *"But Onan, knowing that the child would not be his, spilt his seed on the ground every time he slept with his brother's wife, to avoid producing a child... What he did was offensive to Yahweh (God)"* (Genesis 38:8-10).

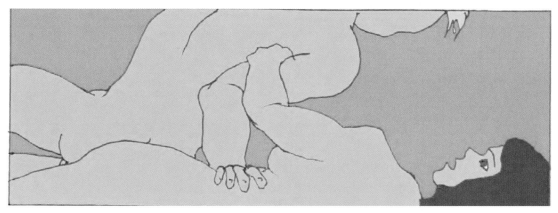

...Which, by the way, is also the reason that masturbation is strictly forbidden for males in Christian cultures. Masturbation has been associated with all sorts of illnesses even after the era of Freud. Philosophers such as Immanuel Kant saw masturbation as a violation of moral law, and Jean Jacques Rousseau called masturbation "mental rape." Only after the Kinsey report (1953) was masturbation regarded to be something perfectly normal and healthy.

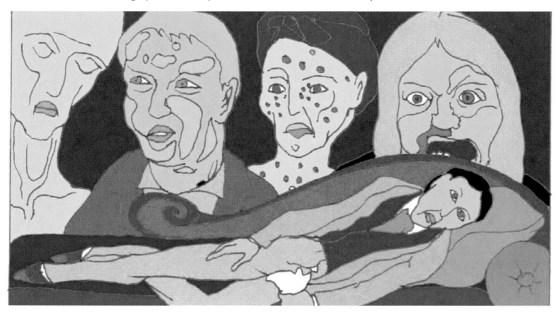

John: Then there is the (in)famous story of **SODOM AND GOMORRAH** in the Bible (Genesis 18). Lot refused to surrender his two angelic male guests to the citizens of Sodom, so that they could sexually abuse and humiliate them.

...Lot offered his two daughters to them instead. But the citizens were not interested. No greater humiliation could the citizens cause than to spill their semen and so destroy any possibility for new life for Lot and his family. Hostility, not hospitality, was the issue of this story.

...Which is why the story of the incest between Lot and his daughters in the Book of Genesis (19:30-38) was not considered to be beyond the pale.

"Lot settled in the hill country with his two daughters... The elder said to the younger, 'Our father is an old man, and there is not a man in the land to marry us in the way they do the world over. Come, let us ply our father with drink and sleep with him; in that way we shall have children by our father.'

"...That night they made their father drunk and the elder...and the younger slept with him... Both daughters became pregnant by their father.

"...The elder gave birth to a son...the ancestor of the Moabites...the younger gave birth to a son...the ancestor of the Bene-ammon of our times."

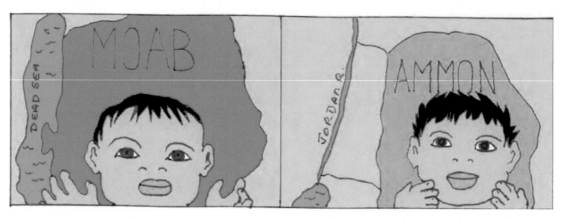

John: The Moabites and the Bene-ammon were looked down upon by the Israelites who had reached the "Promised Land" after forty years wandering in the desert. But that did not take away the legitimacy of the Moabites and Bene-ammon as such.

The fact that women were mere "incubators" for new life that had its exclusive origin with man, was still believed. So, lesbian relationships were of no real import to the people of the Bible. At worst, lesbians were seen and treated as witches, even into the 19th century AD.

Tony: The question still remains, "Are cases of lesbian relationships to be found in the Bible?"

John: The answer is "no" as far as we know. But there are some who suggest that **RUTH AND NAOMI** had a lesbian relationship. The story of Ruth and Naomi...

"A certain man...Elimelech, with his wife Naomi, and his two sons, Mahlon and Chilion...from Bethlehem in Judah, went to the country of Moab and settled there... Elimelech died.

"...The two sons...married Moabite women...Orpah and Ruth.

About ten years later both Mahlon and Chilion died.

"Naomi said to her two daughters-in-law, 'Go back, each of you to your mother's house' ...Orpah kissed her mother-in-law and went back to her people.

"But Ruth said, 'Do not press me to leave you and to turn back from your company. Wherever you go, I will go. Wherever you live, I will live. Your people shall be my people and your God, my God. Wherever you die, I will die and there I shall be buried. May Yahweh do this thing to me and more also, even if death should come between us.'

"...Ruth went with Naomi to Bethlehem in Judah" (Ruth 1–4). There Boaz fell in love with Ruth and married her.

Boaz and Ruth had a son and called him Obed, who was to become the father of Jesse, who was to become the father of King David.

Tony: But did Naomi and Ruth have a lesbian love relationship?

John: We don't know, and nobody at that time would have cared.

John: Let us move to the New Testament section of the Bible. The Gospel According to John is based on the written testimony of a disciple: *"This disciple is the one who vouches for these things and has written them down and we know that his testimony is true"* *(John 21:24).*

John: The words, *"The disciple who Jesus loved,"* is used six times in the Gospel According to John, but not in the other gospels attributed to Matthew, Mark, and Luke.

Since the end of the first century, the **"BELOVED DISCIPLE"** has been commonly/popularly identified with John, one of the twelve chosen apostles.

John: The Last Supper is where the words, "the disciple who Jesus loved" is mentioned and best remembered.

"The disciple who Jesus loved was reclining next to Jesus. Simon Peter signaled to him and said, 'Ask who it is he means.' So leaning back on Jesus' breast, he said, 'Who is it, Lord?'" (John 13: 23-25).

"Seeing his mother and the disciple Jesus loved standing near her" (John 26: 26-27).

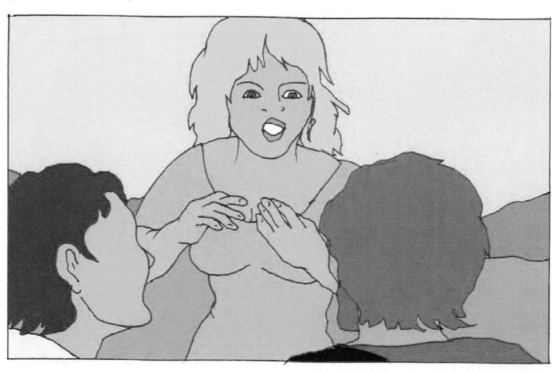

"Mary of Magdala...came running to Simon Peter and the other disciple Jesus loved" (John 20:2).

"So Peter set out with the other disciple to go to the tomb. They ran together, but the other disciple, the one Jesus loved, running faster than Peter, reached the tomb first" (John 20:3-4).

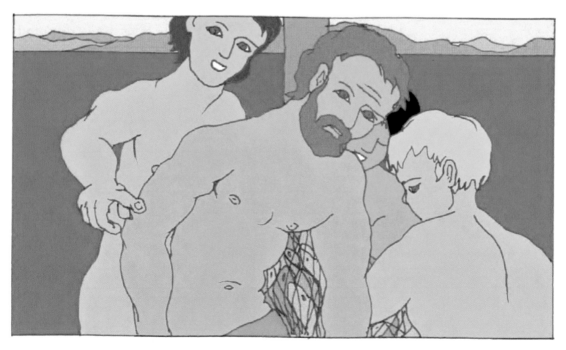

"The disciple who Jesus loved said to Peter, 'It is the Lord.' At these words Peter, who had practically nothing on...

"Peter turned and saw the disciple Jesus loved following them, the one who had leaned on his breast at the supper and had said to him, 'Lord, who is it that will betray you?' Seeing him Peter said to Jesus, 'What about him, Lord?' Jesus answered, 'If I want him to stay behind till I come, what does it matter to you? You are to follow me'" (John 21:20-22).

"The rumor then went out amongst the brothers that this disciple would not die. Yet Jesus had not said to Peter, 'He will not die,' but, 'If I want him to stay behind till I come'" (John 21:23).

John: Some argue that it was not John, but James, the brother of Jesus, that the words "the disciple Jesus loved" refer to.

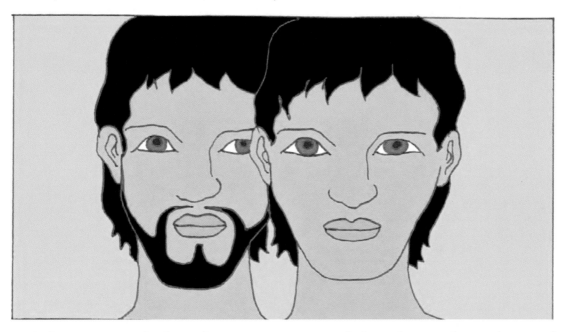

....Others argued that it was Lazarus. "The sisters (Martha and Mary) sent this message to Jesus, 'Lord, the man you love is ill' (John 11:3).

Tony: Why did the writer of the Gospel according to John conceal his identity? Was it for political or security reasons?

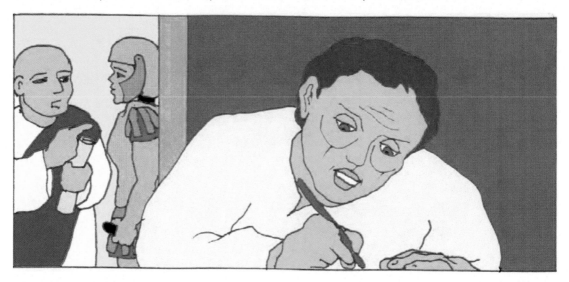

...or to create greater objectivity as narrator of the story?

In art, especially in depictions of the Last Supper, the Beloved Disciple is often portrayed as beardless and as one of the twelve apostles.

...Or with Mary, the mother of Jesus, at the crucifixion.

Tony: In some medieval art the Beloved Disciple is portrayed with his head on Christ's lap as was also shown previously.

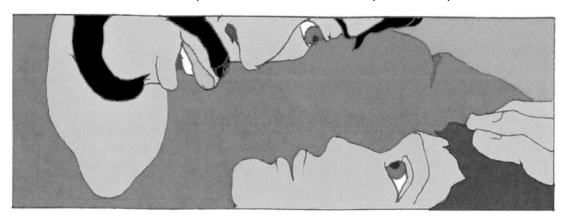

John: It can only be said that the Beloved Disciple was a real historical person, but in the end there is no absolute consensus on who exactly the Beloved Disciple was.

Tony: The claim that the "Beloved Disciple" was homosexual is most probably a case of wishful thinking on the part of some gays...

... and so let us dream on!

John: No, let's rather move on. Have you ever heard of **SERGIUS AND BACCHUS?**

St. Sergius and St. Bacchus were 4th-century Roman soldiers and revered as Christian martyrs by Catholics, Orthodox, and Oriental Orthodox Christians.

John: According to legend, they came from the Roman aristocracy and were appointed officers of the Roman Border Troops in Syria by Emperor Maximianus (285-305).

...When the Emperor Galerius (305-311) was in Arabissus, he went into the temple of Jupiter to make ritual offerings. Sergius and Bacchus refused to go into the temple with him. The emperor suspected that they were secret Christians.

Bacchus and Sergius were arrested. They were first flogged and then forced to wear women's clothes and dragged through the city.

Sergius and Bacchus were tried and tortured in two different places, which seems to suggest that they were taken by the hated Christian-persecutor, Antiochus, on tour through surrounding cities.

It was in Barbalis that Bacchus was flogged to death.

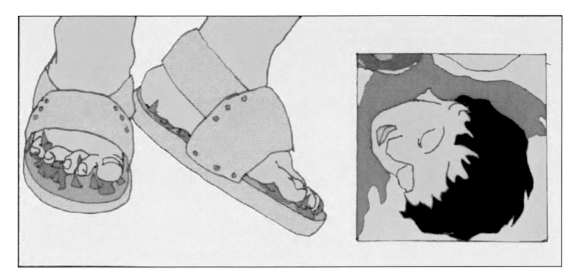

...A short while later Sergius was forced to put on iron shoes with soles covered with sharp nails and then compelled to walk fifteen miles from the city of Resafa into the desert. At the end of that walk, he was beheaded.

Tony: Why have Sergius and Bacchus become "gay icons" today? Nobody knows whether or not they were gay.

John: I think they became "gay icons" not because they were secret Christians, but because the two of them supported each other in their effort to be allowed to believe in themselves and in Christ.

John: Have you ever heard of **BRIGID and DARLUGHDACH**?

Tony: No, never.

John: Here is their story.

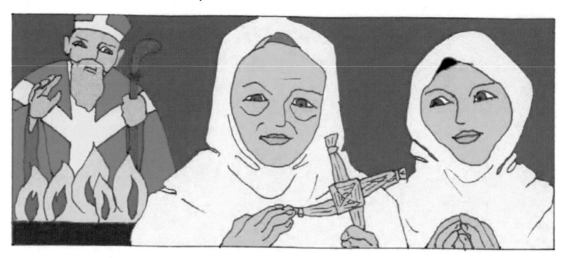

Brigid was born in 451 AD in Faughart, County Louth, Ireland, into slavery. She belonged to a druid, a religious leader and member of a high-ranking class in ancient Celtic culture. She was returned to her father by the druid when she was ten years old.

She was known to be very charitable, donating the belongings of her father to anyone who asked. He was not pleased. The king of Leinster asked her father to release her from slavery and allow her to be a "free" woman.

She was given "the veil" as a nun by St. Mel of Ardagh, and around 480 she founded a monastery at Kildare for communal consecrated religious life for women in Ireland. That was the beginning of many convents all over Ireland.

Brigid shared her bed with Darlughdach. She believed, like many Celtic saints, that each person needs a soul friend to discover together that God speaks most powerfully in the seemingly mundane details of shared daily living.

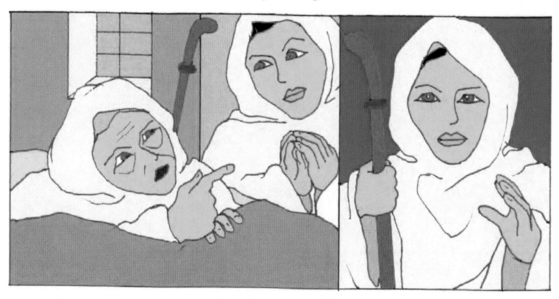

When Brigid lay dying, Darlughdach wished to die with her. But Brigid told her she would have to wait a year. Darlughdach died exactly one year later. Meanwhile, she had succeeded Brigid as Abbess of Kildare, as Brigid had wanted.

Tony: But were they lesbian?

John: Possibly. But we don't know.

John: HILDEGARD VON BINGEN is also a fascinating woman, who many think was lesbian.

Hildegard was born around 1098 in Bermersheim, Germany, of lower nobility.

She was offered by her parents as oblate to the Benedictine Monastery of Disibodenberg. She made her vows, together with Jutta, the daughter of Count Stephan II of Sponheim.

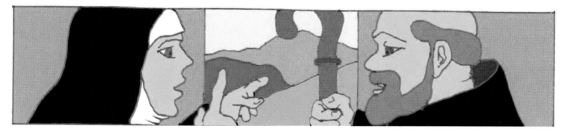

She was asked to become the prioress of the double (male and female) monastery of Disibodenberg.

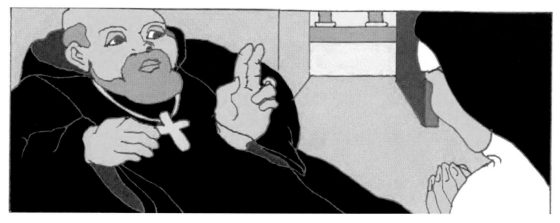

But she wanted to establish a convent exclusively for women at St. Rupensberg in Bingen. The abbot refused. But when he became seriously ill in 1150, he finally relented.

She had a vision very early on in life which she described as *umbra viventis lucis* (the reflection of the living light). In later years, she knew that this gift could not be explained to others. Nevertheless, at the age of 42 she received a vision she believed was an instruction from God *to write down that which you see and hear.* And she did.

She wrote three monumental volumes of visionary theology: 1. *Scivias*, (know the ways of the Lord–sci-vias-domini) to which Pope Eugenius III gave his blessing at the Synod of Trier. 2. *Liber Vitae Meritorum* (dramatic confrontations between virtues and vices) and 3. *Liber Divinorum Operum* (10 visions, cosmic in scale, to illustrate the relationship between God and his creation.)

She wrote musical compositions for use in the liturgy, and a musical morality play (*Ordo Virtutem*). She also left scientific and medicinal writings not rooted in visionary experiences.

In recent years she has become of particular interest to feminist scholars. And some say that she was lesbian because of her strong emotional attachment to women and in particular to her personal assistant Richardis von Stade.

Richardis was fluent in Latin, but unlike Hildegard, was not herself a mystic. She was made abbess of the convent in Bassum, much against the wishes of Hildegard. There she died one year later in 1152.

John: But of course we don't know whether Hildegard and/or Richardis von Stade were lesbian.

John: We move on now to **AELRED OF RIEVAULX** (1110 – 1167)

Aelred was the son of Eilaf, priest of St. Andrew's Parish, Hexham, Northumbria, England.

Aelred worked at the Court of King David of Scotland. His best known book is *De Spirituali Amicitia* (Spiritual Friendship). In it, he tells of his early adolescence with his "speaker" (a form of "dialogue" he used). *"The charm of my companions gave me the greatest pleasure. Among the usual faults that often endanger youth, my mind surrendered wholly to affection and became elevated to love. Nothing is more valuable than to be loved and to love."*

He became a monk at the Cistercian Abbey of Rievaulx, in Yorkshire, England in 1134. He was eventually elected as abbot of that same abbey in 1147.

He developed a Theology of Friendship: *"Just as there is a continuous dialogue and interchange of love between the three persons of the Trinity, so human beings–rational creatures, made in the image and likeness of this Trinity of Persons–are called to relationships based on mutual dialogue, exchange, sharing and self-giving."*

The most quoted passage from *Spiritual Friendship* is:

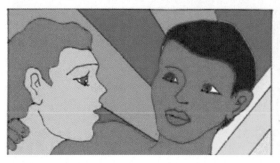 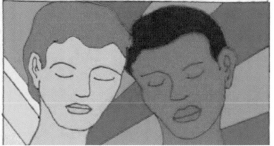

(1) It is no small consolation in this life to have someone who can unite with you in an intimate affection and the embrace of a holy love,

(2) someone in whom your spirit can rest,

 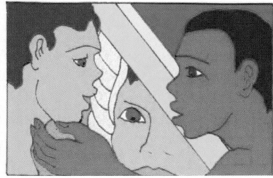

(3) to whom you can pour out your soul,

(4) to whose pleasant exchanges, as to soothing songs you can fly in sorrow...

 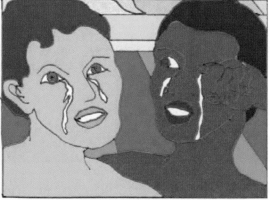

(5) with whose spiritual kisses, as with remedial salves, you may draw out all the weariness of your restless anxieties, (6) a man who can shed tears with you in your worries,

(7) ...be happy with you when things go well, (8) search out with you the answers to your problems,

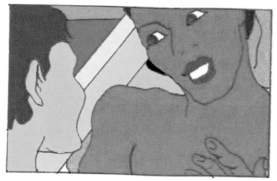

(9) ...whom, with the ties of charity you can lead into the depths of your heart...(10) where sweetness of the spirit flows between you,

(11) where you can so join yourself and cleave to him that soul mingles with soul and two become one.

Aelred died on January 12, 1167. Many think that Aelred was homosexual. However, he did exhort chastity among the unmarried, condemning as sinful sexual relationships and activity outside of marriage.

Tony: I believe that **JOAN OF ARC** is popularly assumed to have been lesbian, or perhaps even transgender. Her story:

Joan of Arc was born at Domrémy in France in 1412. She had dreams/visions from about the age of 13, seeing figures such as St. Michael the Archangel, Saint Catherine and St. Margaret, who told her to drive out the English and take the Dauphin (crown prince of France) to Rheims to be crowned king. She said she cried when they left because they were so beautiful.

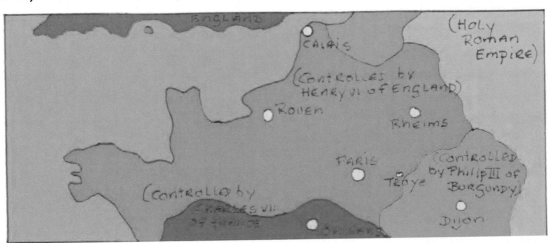

When she began to influence events in 1429 AD, nearly the whole of northern France, and some parts of the southwest, were under Anglo-Burgundian control. The English controlled Paris; the Burgundian faction controlled Rheims (the traditional site for the coronation of French kings) together with the English.

At age 16 she wanted to be escorted to the French Royal Court at Chinon, but was refused. A year later she tried again and succeeded with the help of two soldiers, Jean de Metz and Bertrand de Poulengy. *"I must be at the king's side...there will be no help (for the kingdom)."* She made the journey disguised as a male soldier.

She met the Dauphin, Charles (he was then 26 years old) at Poitiers. He made background enquiries and a theological examination to verify her morality and confirm that she was not a witch. She was declared to be of irreproachable conduct and a good Christian.

She carried the banner at the battle of Orleans that reclaimed Orleans for the French. She never actually killed anyone.

This was followed by the crowning of Charles VII as King of France at Rheims. Joan was present at the coronation.

The truce with England came to an end. Fighting resumed and Joan was wounded, captured at Compiege by Burgundian troops loyal to the English, and brought to Rouen.

There she was tried for "heresy"; a ploy by the English Crown to get rid of a bizarre prisoner of war with maximum embarrassment to their enemies. Heresy was a capital crime for a repeat offence—and the crime in this case was "Cross-dressing."

She was condemned to death and executed by burning on May 30, 1431. Joan was only 19 years old.

She was posthumously retried with the authorization of Pope Callixtus III in 1455 and declared innocent on July 7, 1456. She was canonized as a saint in the Catholic Church on May 16, 1920.

She was declared a national symbol of France by Napoleon Bonaparte in 1803. She has remained a popular figure in literature, painting, sculpture, and other cultural works.

John: But was she lesbian because she wore men's clothes? Most unlikely. Did she really want to be a boy, a transgender? We'll never know.

Tony: Of course, the term **transgender** is used for someone whose gender identity or expression does not coincide with what was decided at birth, and has various gradations ranging from cross-dressing, transvestite, or androgynous. When the change in sexual identity has been achieved through medical treatment, then we speak of transsexuality.

He feels like ....a she............and she feels like...a he.............

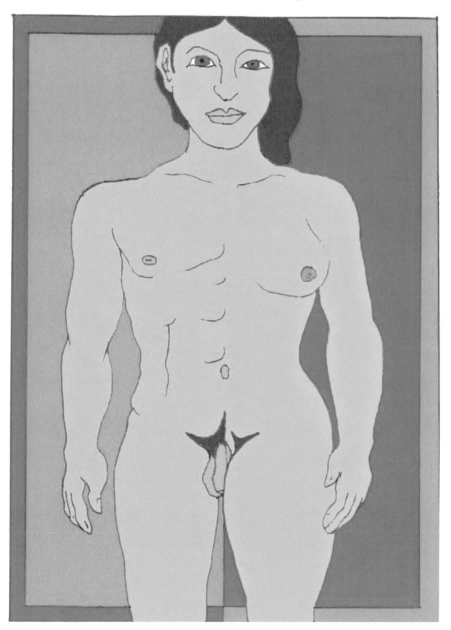

The term transgender began to be used from around 1980 onwards.

John: Now here is someone you have probably never heard of: **SAINT WALATTA PETROS** (1592–1642).

Walatta was born into a noble Abyssinian family and became a saint of the Ethiopian Orthodox Tewahedo Church, formally established in the 4th century, but tracing its origins to the Ethiopian eunuch baptised by Philip, the apostle of Jesus (Acts 8:26-40).

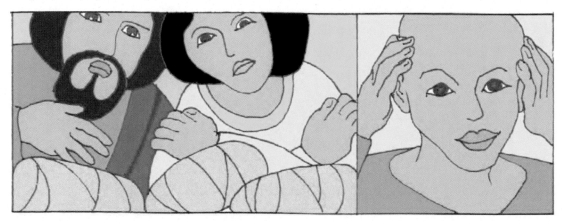

She married one of King Susenyos' counselors at a very young age. This king was privately converted to Catholicism by Portuguese Jesuits. She gave birth to three children—all of whom died.

She then shaved her head and decided to become a nun. But not a Roman Catholic nun. She remained true to the Ethiopian Orthodox Church.

She founded seven religious communities of nuns, the first in Sudan, and then the rest around the large Ethiopian Lake Tana. It is recorded that she was a fierce female leader who did not suffer fools and conquering kings gladly, and that she was much loved.

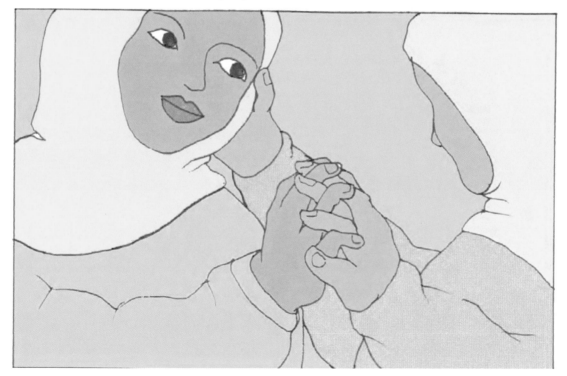

Her biography, written by one of her disciples just thirty years after her death, contains the earliest known depiction of same-sex desire among women in Sub-Saharan-Africa. That section of the text was censored until 2015.

It records that *"as soon as our holy mother Walatta Petros and Eheta Kristos saw each other from afar, love was infused into both their hearts, love for one another, and...they were like people who had known each other beforehand because the Holy Spirit united them."*

After two decades as a nun, Walatta became ill and appointed Eheta Kristos as her successor to head the religious community. *"Upon her deathbed Walatta Petros' last thoughts and words were about her friend, worrying how Eheta would fare without her, saying three times, 'She will be disconsolate; she has no other hope than me.'"*

John: Another extraordinary nun was **SOR JUANA INES DE LA CRUZ** (1648 – 1695).

She was born near Mexico City, on November 12, 1648 as the illegitimate child of a Spanish captain and a criolla (a Latin American of Spanish descent).

She was very intelligent. By the age of three she is reported to have been able to read and write Latin. At eight, she composed a poem on the Eucharist.

At age sixteen, she went to live in Mexico City. She disguised herself as a male student in order to get into the university there, but failed. She continued her studies privately, and became a lady-in-waiting at the court of the colonial viceroy.

In 1667 she entered the Discalced Carmelite Monastery of St. Joseph, but later moved to the Hieronymite nuns, who lived by a more relaxed rule. This made it possible for her to study with no fixed occupations.

She challenged the hierarchical structures of religious authorities in her writings (*Carta Atenagórica*) and advocated a woman's right to formal education. *"One can perfectly well philosophize while cooking supper."*

It was suggested in the 1999 historical novel, *Sor Juana's Second Dream,* by Alicia Gaspar de Alba, that the convent was a place where having sexual relations with other women was socially acceptable.

The archbishop of Mexico, Francisco de Aquiar y Seijas, and other high-ranking officials condemned her for "waywardness." She stopped writing, fearing official censure.

She died on April 17, 1695 while ministering to other nuns stricken during a plague. Scholars interpret her as being a feminist before the time of feminism.

Tony: So far we have looked at people who are presumed to have been gay. Let us now look at people who we know for certain were gay.

John: Yes. And I want to start with **ALAN TURING** (1912–1954).

Alan Turing was born in London, England on June 23, 1912.

He was quite a genius. As a child he read the book, *Natural Wonders Every Child Should Know*, which had a great influence on him. At Cambridge University he studied mathematics.

"Is the answer to a logical question always true?" In 1936 he answered, "No—depending on the circumstances" (*The Church-Turing Thesis*). On the basis of that insight he developed the "Logical Computing Machine."

During the Second World War he worked in secret at the "Government Code and Cipher School" in the grounds of Bletchley Park.

Together with others, he invented the Bombe, a decoding machine capable of deciphering the Enigma Code, the key to the Nazi code system. Turing's efforts contributed enormously to the victory of the allies over Nazi Germany. He was awarded the title, "Officer of the Order of the British Empire," and was chosen to be a member of the prestigious Royal Society in 1951.

After the war he worked as Deputy Director of the computing laboratory at Manchester University. At the same time, he continued working in secret for the Government Code and Cipher Headquarters, until he was excluded on account of his homosexuality in 1948.

In 1952 he was arrested for homosexual activities, a crime in the English legal system until it was scrapped in 1967.

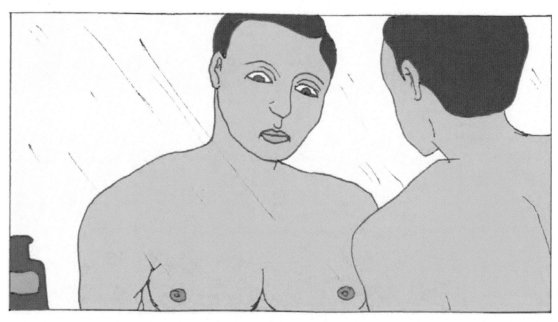

He could choose between undergoing experimental chemical castration or a year's imprisonment. He chose the first. The hormone injections he had been forced to accept led, among other things, to breast formation, which he was not happy about.

On June 7, 1954, he was found dead with an apple in his hand, an apple poisoned with cyanide. It was declared to have been suicide, but that is still under dispute.

On December 24, 2013, Queen Elizabeth II granted Alan Turing a honorable posthumous rehabilitation. His conviction on account of homosexuality was scrapped from the books.

To honor Turing, the Bank of England in 2021 unveiled a new design for its fifty-pound banknote that featured Turing's portrait.

Tony: Let me now tell you about **HARVEY MILK** (1930–1978).

Harvey Milk was born on May 22, 1930 in Woodmere, New York, USA. He was the second son of Lithuanian Jewish parents.

After graduating from the New York State College for Teachers in Albany, he joined the US Navy for the duration of the Korean war. He left the Navy in 1955.

While working as a teacher on Long Island, he met Joe Campbell, with whom he lived for six years.

He kept his early romantic life separate from his parents and work. He was not open about his sexuality, neither was he active in public affairs until he was 40 years old.

He drifted to San Francisco, to Texas, to New York without a steady job or plan.

Harvey met Scott Smith, 18 years younger than himself. He moved once again to San Francisco. There he became more interested in politics and civic matters.

Harvey was elected to the Board of Supervisors in San Francisco and supported Gay Liberation activities in the city. He also had a new lover, Jack Lira. Sadly, Jack committed suicide on August 28, 1978.

And then, two months later, on November 27, 1978, Dan White, a former member of the Board of Supervisors and a known homophobe who had often clashed with Milk, shot Harvey just minutes after he shot the Mayor of San Francisco, George Moscone.

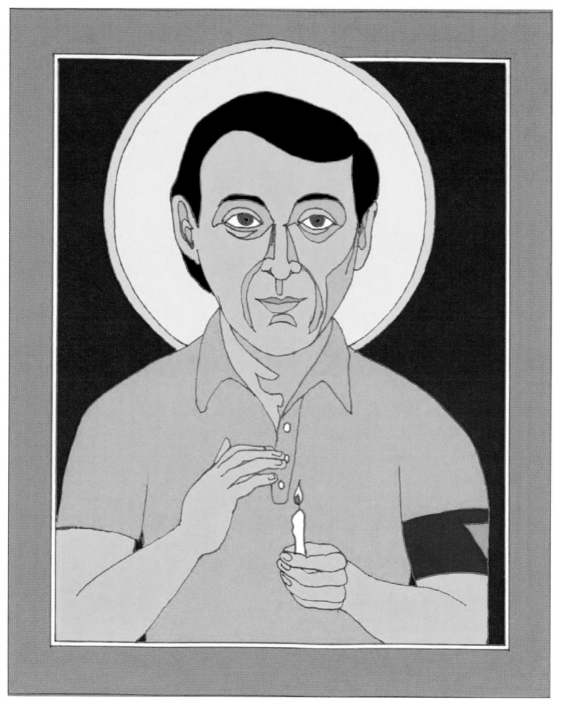

Harvey Milk has become an icon for civil rights movements and Gay Liberation.

John: Let me introduce you to **GEORGE DUNCAN**, (1930–1972).

Tony: Let's hear it, then.

George Duncan was born on July 20, 1930 in London, England. When he was seven years old, he moved with his parents, both from New Zealand, to Melbourne, Australia.

George completed his Melbourne Grammar School education in 1947. From there he moved on to the University of Melbourne, where he studied Philology (the study of language using classic or historic texts). However, his studies were interrupted after he contracted tuberculosis in 1950.

George entered St. John's College, Cambridge, England, where in 1964 he obtained a Ph.D. in Law. After this, he taught Law part-time at the University of Bristol.

He returned to Australia in 1972 to take up a lectureship in Law at the University of Adelaide.

Six weeks after his move to Adelaide, Australia, George and a man called Roger James were sitting together on the bank of the River Torrens (or "Number 1 Beat" as it was then known). This was a popular place for gay or bisexual men to meet. Homosexuality at that time was still illegal in Australia.

George, Roger, and an unknown third man were thrown into the river by a group of men. George, unable to swim, drowned. Roger broke an ankle.

Roger James and other witnesses declined to identify the attackers out of fear for their lives.

The group of men suspected of being George's murderers were three senior vice-squad officers. They were never prosecuted due to lack of witness testimony.

The murder attracted national media coverage and outrage.

Tony: This is the story of **MATTHEW SHEPARD.** (1976–1998)

Matthew Shepard was born on December 1, 1976 in Casper, Wyoming, USA.

He had a younger brother called Logan. The two of them had a very close relationship.

In 1998 his parents moved to Saudi Arabia, staying at the Aramco Residential Camp in Dhahran. Meanwhile, Matthew attended the American School in Switzerland. He graduated there in 1995.

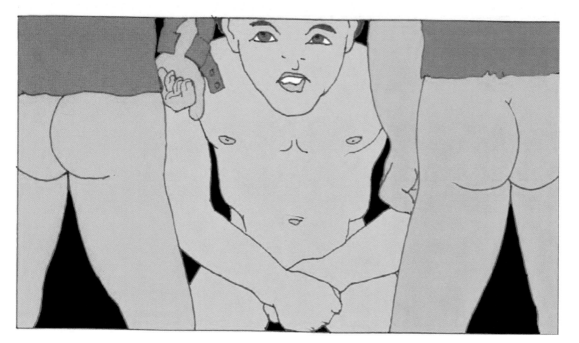

In 1995, Matthew was beaten and raped during a high school trip to Morocco. As a result, he suffered bouts of depression and panic attacks. He was hospitalized on a number of occasions. One of his friends feared that his depression drove him to take drugs during college.

He became a first-year political science major at the University of Wyoming in Laramie and was chosen to be a student representative to the Wyoming Environmental Council.

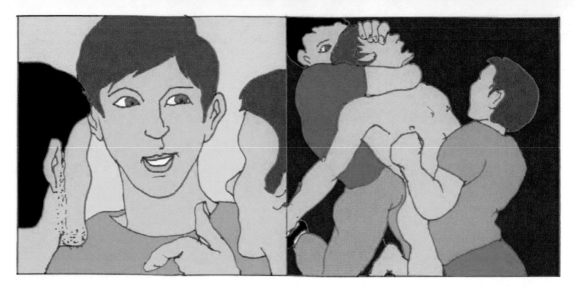

On the night of October 6, 1998, he was approached by Aaron McKinney and Russell Henderson at the Fireside Lounge in Laramie. Claiming they were gay, they lured him to leave with them and drive out to the eastern edge of town. There, one of them beat him brutally and then the other tied him to a nearby fence. There they left him.

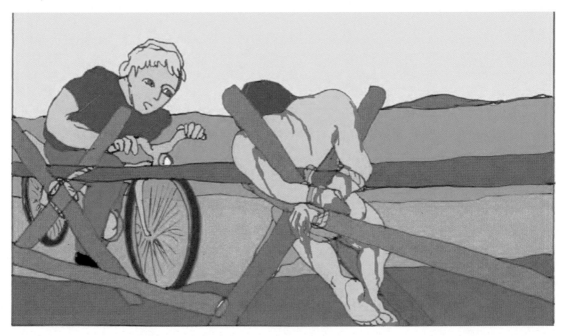

Matthew was found eighteen hours later by a mountain biker, who initially mistook him for a scarecrow.

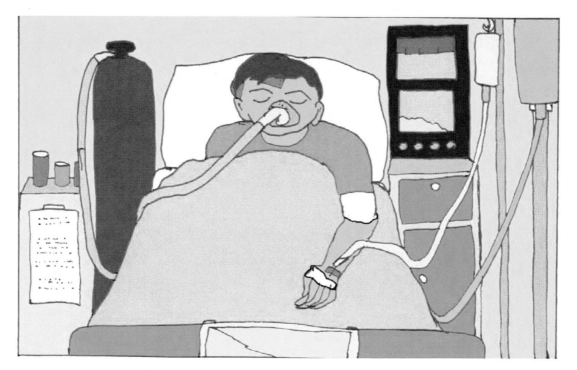

He was rescued and brought to Poudre Valley Hospital, where he died five days later, on October 12, 1998. He never recovered consciousness. He was 21 years old. While he was in the hospital it was discovered that he had AIDS.

McKinney and Henderson were arrested and initially charged with attempted murder, kidnapping, and aggravated robbery. Later they were charged with first degree murder.

The jury found McKinney not guilty of premeditated murder, but guilty of felony murder. Henderson pleaded guilty to murder and kidnapping charges to avoid the death penalty. Both of them were given two consecutive life sentences.

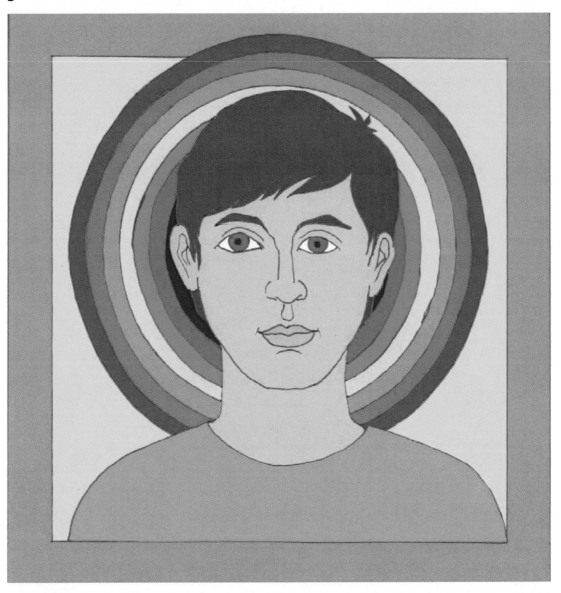

Was Matthew Shepard's murder a "hate crime"? Was he murdered because he was gay? The murderers denied it. However, it did lead to hate crime legislation signed into law by President Obama on October 28, 2009.

Matthew Shepard—martyr and the icon for victims of gay-bashing.

John: There is another American homo I would like to draw your attention to.

Tony: Who?

John: MYCHAL JUDGE (1933–2001)

Mychal Judge, the first born of a pair of fraternal twins, was born on May 11, 1933 in Brooklyn, New York. His twin sister Dympna was born two days later.

He joined the Order of the Friars Minor (Franciscans). In 1955 he took his vows as a Franciscan. He was ordained a priest in 1961.

He served several parishes, and in 1986 was assigned to the St. Francis of Assisi Catholic Church in Manhattan, where he had originally come into contact with the Franciscans. He lived and worked from there until he died.

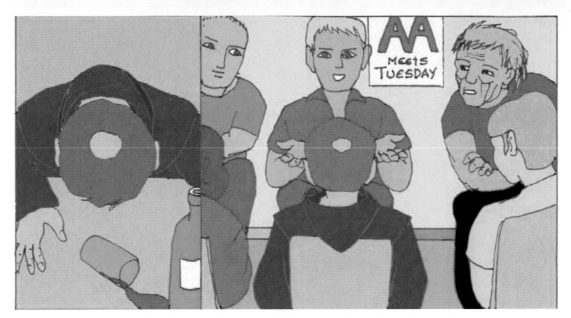

Somewhere around 1971, he became an alcoholic. With the support of Alcoholics Anonymous, he sobered up and continued to share his story of alcoholism and recovery with others.

In 1992 he was appointed as chaplain to the New York Fire Department. As such he offered encouragement and prayers at fires, rescues, and hospital visits. He also counseled firemen and their families.

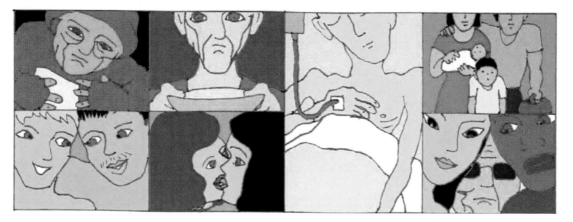

Mychal was also well known in the city for his ministry to the homeless, hungry, people with AIDS, immigrants, gays and lesbians, and those marginalized by society.

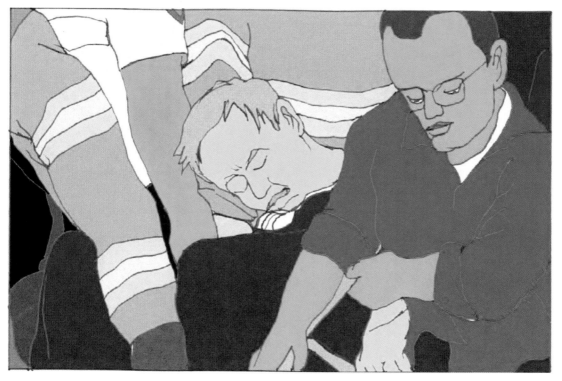

On 9/11, the World Trade Center was hit by two airliners and caught fire. Mychal rushed to the site. He entered the lobby of the World Trade Center North Tower. When the neighboring South Tower collapsed, the debris went flying through the North Tower lobby, killing many inside, including Mychal Judge. His body was recovered and carried out by five firemen. This event was photographed. It became one of the most famous images relating to 9/11.

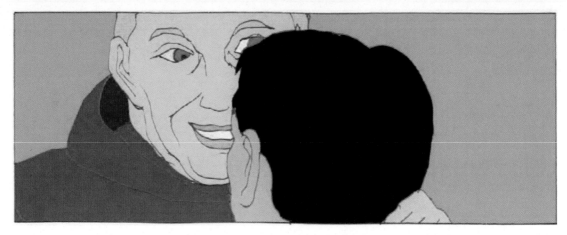

Following his death, friends and associates revealed that Mychal Judge was gay. He had developed a romantic relationship with a Filipino nurse named Al Alvarado during the last year of his life.

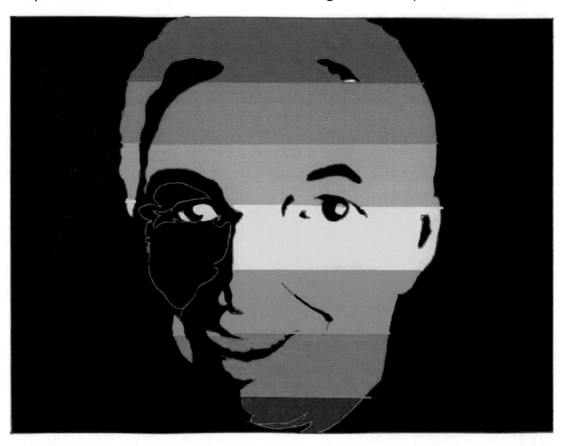

He had also been a long term member of "Dignity," a Catholic activist organization that advocates change in the Catholic Church's teaching on homosexuality.

Tony: Have you ever heard of **FANNY ANN EDDY** (1974-2004)?

John: No.

Tony: Well, most people haven't.

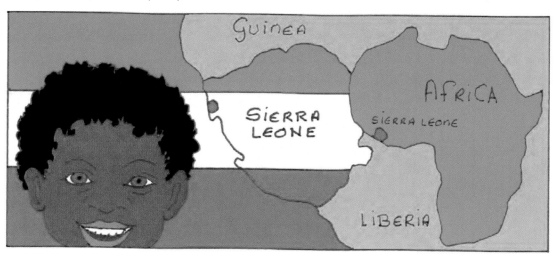

Fanny Ann Eddy was born on June 14, 1974 in Sierra Leone.

Between 1991 and 2002 Sierra Leone was engaged in a violent civil war. This forced her to leave the country and live in a refugee camp.

She fought to have the needs of her community attended to. She was a charismatic person and a good friend to many. She returned to Sierra Leone in 2002.

On her return, she founded the SLLGA (Sierra Leone Lesbian and Gay Association), the first organization of its kind in the country. She worked to fight the laws that denied queer identities, focusing, for instance, on the difference between the treatment of "queer criminals" and "heterosexual criminals."

She addressed the United Nations Commission on Human Rights in 2004 and stated that there were LGBTQ people throughout Africa, but that they live in fear.

"Silence creates vulnerability. You members of the Commission on Human Rights can break the silence. You can acknowledge that we exist, throughout Africa and on every continent, and that human rights violations based on sexual orientation or gender identity are committed every day. You can help us combat those violations and achieve our full rights and freedoms in every society, including our beloved Sierra Leone."

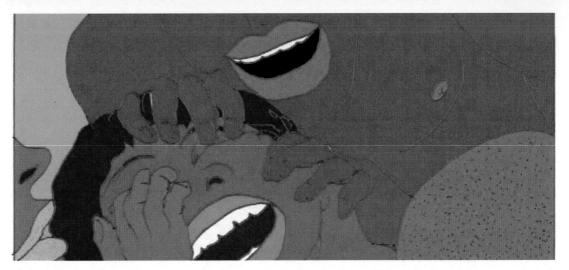

On the September 29, 2004, a group of at least three men broke into the office of the SLLGA in central Freetown. They gang-raped Fanny Ann. They stabbed her and broke her neck. The police caught one of the men, but he escaped. The police never treated it as a hate crime.

Fanny Ann Eddy was survived by a partner, Esther Chikalipa and a ten-year-old son. The Hirschfield Eddy Foundation in Berlin, Germany was founded in 2007, honoring her memory and that of Hirschfield by focusing on the human rights of Gay, Lesbian, Bisexual, and Transgender people.

John: I want to introduce you to someone whose life did not end in tragedy, namely **MARY DALY** (1928-2010).

Mary Daly was born on October 16, 1928 in Schenectady, New York. She was baptized and enjoyed a Catholic upbringing. Early in her childhood, she claimed to have had mystical experiences in which she felt the presence of divinity in nature.

She obtained two doctorates in Sacred Theology and Philosophy from the University of Fribourg, Switzerland, a master's degree in English from the Catholic University of America, and a doctorate in Religion from St. Mary's College, Indiana, USA.

From 1967 to 1999 she taught courses in theology, feminist ethics and patriarchy (a social system in which political, moral, and financial power is primarily the privilege of men) at Boston College, a private Jesuit Research University in Chestnut Hill, Massachusetts.

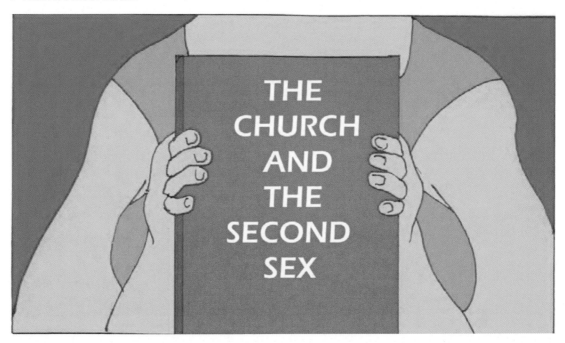

She was threatened with dismissal following the publication of her first book, *The Church and the Second Sex*. With student support, she was eventually granted tenure (the right to keep your professorship for as long as you want it, regardless of politics or unorthodox beliefs).

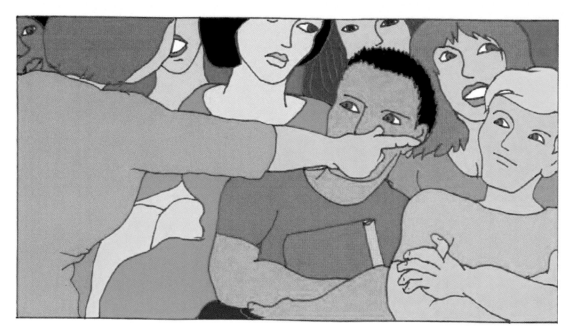

In some of her classes, she refused to admit male students, *saying that "their presence inhibited class discussion."* In 1998 her rights to tenure were removed by the college, following a "discrimination claim" by two male students. A confidential out-of-court settlement was reached. She documented these events in 2006 in her book, *Amazon Grace: Re-Calling the Courage to Sin Big.*

She published a number of books. Her best known is *Beyond God the Father* (1973). It is regarded as a foundational work in feminist theology. She argued that Christian theology is a "totem" of patriarchy, and therefore inherently oppressive towards women. She saw the Catholic Church as fundamentally corrupt.

She wrote about what she called Gyn/Ecology, a sort of 'female energy' which is linked to the essential life-creating condition of the female spirit/body. She claimed in an interview in 1999 that men should be eliminated to save nature. *"I don't think about men. I really don't care about them."*

She came out as lesbian in the early 1970's. She died at the age of 81 on January 3, 2010 in Gardner, Massachusetts, USA.

Tony: Do you know of any more contemporary African heavenly homos?

John: Yes, certainly. **DAVID KATO** (1964 – 2011).

David Kato, a member of the Kisulu clan, was born on February 13, 1964 in Mukono, Uganda. He was named Kato because he was the younger of twins. He was educated at Kings College, Buda and the Kyambogo University.

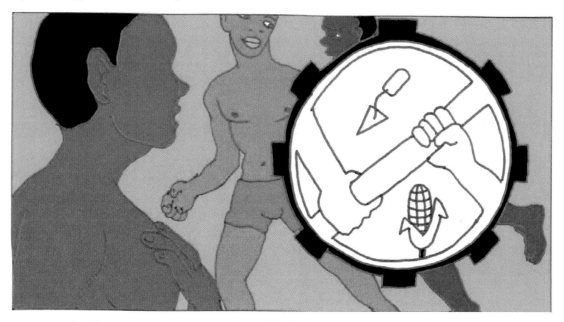

He taught in various schools, including the Nile Vocational Institute in Njeru near Jinja. It is there that he became aware of his sexual orientation. He was subsequently dismissed without any benefits in 1991. Later on, he came out to his twin brother, John.

He left to teach in Johannesburg, South Africa, which was then in transition from Apartheid to a multiracial democracy.

He returned to Uganda in 1998. He decided to come out publicly as being gay at a press conference. He was arrested and held in police custody, but released not long afterwards.

He continued to maintain contact with pro-LGBT activists outside of his country.

In 2002 he became a teacher at the St. Herman Nkoni Boys Primary School, Masaka District. Meanwhile he also became highly involved with the underground LGBT rights movement in Uganda and was a founding member of SMUG (Sexual Minorities Uganda) in 2004.

He spoke at a United Nations-funded Consultative Conference on Human Rights on the anti-LGBT atmosphere in Uganda (during which some members openly joked and snickered). A rumor circulated that David Bahati, a member of parliament, had ordered Kato and other members of SMUG to be arrested. Kato left the conference immediately. Meanwhile Bahati went into a tirade against homosexuality at that same conference.

By 2010 he had resigned his job as a school teacher in order to focus on his work for SMUG. He was one of the 100 persons whose names and photos were published in the Ugandan newspaper *Rolling Stone* in an article that called for their execution as homosexuals. Kato and two others sued the newspaper to force it to stop publishing names and pictures of people believed to be gay or lesbian. The court ordered the paper to pay Kato and his fellow plaintiffs 1,500 Ugandan shillings (approximately US$ 600).

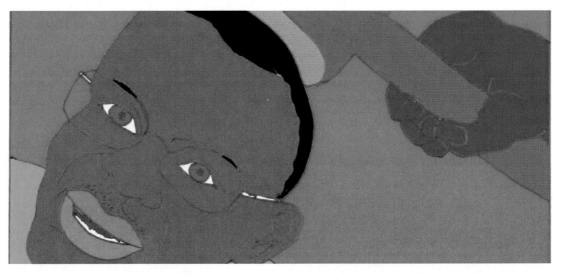

On January 26, around 14:00, he was attacked in his home by a man who hit him twice on the head with a hammer. The attacker fled on foot. Kato died on his way to Kawolo General Hospital. The Christian preacher Thomas Musoke spoke at Kato's funeral against gays and lesbians. He was forced from the pulpit by those present.

The Ugandan Minister for Ethics and Integrity, James Nsaba Buturo is on record as having said, *"Homosexuals can forget about human rights."* Since then things have not changed in Uganda.

Tony: Now I would like to tell you about two gay men from Bangladesh, namely **XULHAZ MANNAN** (1976–2016) and **MAHBUB RABBI TONOY** (?–2016).

Xulhaz Mannan was born on April 26, 1976. (Mahbub Tonoy's birth date is not known by the author). Xulhaz obtained a master's degree in Social Sciences and Conflict Studies from Dhaka University in 2003.

He started work with the MGH group (a Dutch Mediation group offering mediation in private to companies and organizations). At a later date he joined the US embassy in Dhakar as protocol ambassador. In September 2015 he switched to USAID.

Xulhaz founded and published the only magazine for the LGBT community in Bangladesh, *Roopbaan*, in 2014. Mahbub became its first secretary-general.

Mahbub Rabbi Tonoy was a volunteer with *Boys of Bangladesh*, a gay male platform. He saw himself as a theater artist and children's drama trainer. He loved acting, social work, fun, travelling, books, movies, romance...

The two of them were involved in organizing the Rainbow Rally in Dhakar in April, 2014.

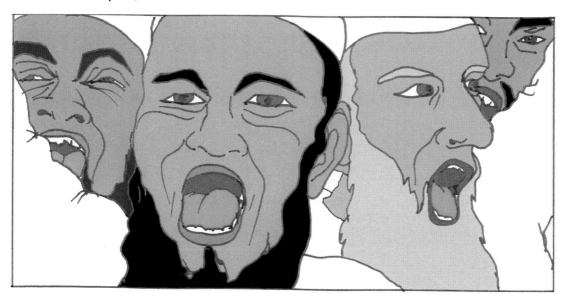

In 2016, the Rainbow Rally was canceled by the police because Islamic groups had threatened to kill anyone taking part. The Bangladesh Prime Minister, Sheikh Hasina, criticized the writings of Xulhaz, comparing them with pornography.

On Monday evening, on April 25, 2016, Xulhaz and Mahbub were together in Xulhaz's apartment when a group of Islamist extremists burst in and slashed them to death, shouting "Allahu Akbar" (Allah is great).

Minhaz Mannan, Xulhaz's brother, said, "Xulhaz was a lover of life, as was Mahbub. Xulhaz didn't die. I find his soul everywhere. He is still alive in the rivers and the green fields of Bangladesh."

Tony: We started this conversation on "heavenly homos," and included lesbians and transgendered people. Also the "LGBT(Q) community" has been mentioned several times. The B stands for Bisexuals, but they have not come into the picture so far.

John: Are you sure? If David and Jonathan had been sexually attracted to each other while they were married to their wives, they would surely qualify as bisexuals. But of course we know that that is probably a case of wishful thinking on the part of the LGBT community.

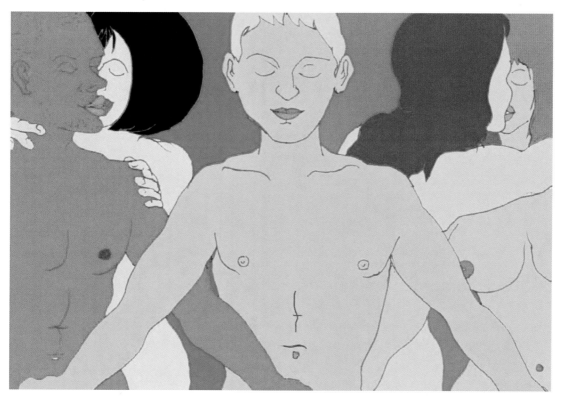

The term **BISEXUALITY** is mainly used in the context of human attraction to denote romantic or sexual feelings towards both men and women. A bisexual identity does not necessarily equate to equal sexual attraction to both sexes. And scientists do not know the exact cause of bisexual orientation, but theorize that it is caused by a complex interplay of genetic, hormonal, and environmental influences. They do not view it as a free choice.

Tony: Have you ever heard of the play, "Who's Afraid of Virginia Woolf?" by Edward Albee? The real **VIRGINIA WOOLF** (1882–1941) was bisexual.

She was born Adeline Virginia Stephen in South Kensington, London, England on January 25, 1882, into an affluent family, the seventh of eight children.

Her mother died in 1895 when Virginia was just 13 years old. This caused her to experience her first mental breakdown. Her father's death in 1904 was followed by another mental breakdown.

She suffered many such breakdowns during the course of her life.

She studied classics and history at the Ladies Department of King's College, London. She began writing professionally in 1900.

She married Leonard Woolf in 1912. Together they founded the Hogarth Press, which also published her books.

Of her early life in South Kensington she wrote, *"22 Hyde Park Gate was divided curiously—downstairs there was pure convention; upstairs, pure intellect."* Her priority in life was to escape from Victorian conventionality.

And she certainly did that as far as her sexuality was concerned. She had a sexual relationship with Vita Sackville-West and she also bragged of her sexual affairs with other women.

Virginia was devoted to her husband Leonard Woolf, who knew of her affairs with women.

28th March 1941

Dearest, I feel certa

Virginia Woolf died by drowning herself in the River Ouse at Lewes. She was 59 years old. She had put stones in her pockets.

In the suicide note addressed to her husband, she wrote: *"Dearest, I feel certain I am going mad again... I shan't recover this time... I owe all the happiness of my life to you... I don't think two people could have been happier than we have been."*

John: We began by looking at 'Heavenly Homos' and soon agreed that our subject includes "heavenly" lesbians, gays, bisexuals, and transgendered people, as the letters LGBT are now commonly used to indicate them...

...But now I hear that there are some people and organizations that want to extend that list with "p" and "a"—"p" referring to pansexuals and "a" referring to asexuals.

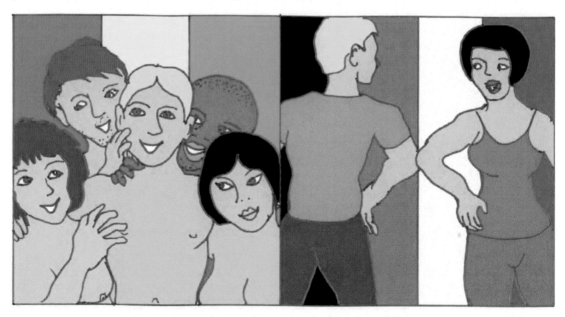

Tony: Let us not do that. There is much discussion about the inclusiveness and exclusiveness such categorization brings with it. These categories, viz. "**PANSEXUALITY**" and "**ASEXUALITY**" have only come to the fore recently and are still fluid concepts, especially as regards their human rights status.

John: You are right. The difference, for instance, between bisexuality and pansexuality seems somewhat arbitrary. But one could make a case for "asexuality."

Tony: How so?

John: "Asexual" describes people who feel no sexual attraction. No one knows why they feel no attraction.

Tony: Could it be because of trauma?

John: There are persons who define themselves as being asexuals who have been gang raped. But were they gang raped because of their assumed or asserted "asexuality," or for other reasons? For instance were alcohol or drugs involved? Was it an anonymous attack or deliberate, and so on and so forth...

...What is the origin of their perception of themselves as being asexual, and how permanent is this? The answers to these questions are still being sought, whereas the questions regarding homosexuality and lesbianism, bisexuality and transgenderism have been answered to a large extent and accepted—although not necessarily to the satisfaction of everybody. But that is another story.

Tony: I think we have covered enough stories of "past" homos and lesbians, bisexuals, and transgendered people. And I agree with you, they are "heavenly" no matter how you wish to define "heaven."

John: You are right. But allow me to introduce you to one last person, whose sexual orientation was probably heterosexual, though that has not been established with any certainty. However, he has become an icon for all persons seeking positive affirmation of their sexuality, however perceived.

John: His name is **JAN VAN KILSDONK** (1917-2008)

Jan van Kilsdonk was born on March 19, 1917, in Zeeland, Brabant, the Netherlands. He joined the Jesuits (the Society of Jesus) in 1934 and was ordained a priest on August 22, 1945.

His first priestly appointment was as chaplain to ex-NSB (people who had collaborated with the Nazi occupiers of the Netherlands during World War II). There he developed a profound respect for marginalized and suffering people.

From 1947 until 1960 he taught religion at the St. Ignatius Jesuit College in Amsterdam. After that he was appointed chaplain to the St. Thomas Aquinas Student Society in Amsterdam. He remained their chaplain until 1982.

Jan Van Kilsdonk started the Amsterdam *Studentenekklesia* in 1960. He came into conflict with the bishop of Haarlem, Mgr. Zwartkruis, concerning the meaning of the eucharist and celibacy. However he remained celibate and Jesuit and loyal to his colleagues at the *Studentenekklesia*, viz. Huub Oosterhuis and Jos Vrijburg , both former Jesuit priests.

Pastorally Jan van Kilsdonk focused on meeting with young people, particularly men who had little or no connection with a church, and often had complicated relationships at home. He became more and more pastorally involved with gays. When AIDS affected young men, he was there for them. He ignored the Catholic Church prohibition on the use of condoms.

He visited his "clients" in student flats, pubs, and gay clubs in Amsterdam, and continued doing this even after his official retirement as student chaplain in 1982.

He died in his sleep at home in Amsterdam, on July 1, 2008, at 91 years old.

John: His most famous words as far as I am concerned were, *"Homosexuality is a unique inspiration of the Creator"* (*Homosexualiteit is een vondst van de Schepper*).

Tony: I like that. I think that is a brilliant description of the homosexual condition—of homosexuality.

Tony: ...and so I suggest that we end this "Heavenly Homos Etc." reflection with a quote I came across recently. It is from **DANELL LEYVA**. He came from Cuba and was an Olympic and World Gymnastics Champion in London (2012) and Rio de Janeiro (2016). When he finally realized he wasn't straight (heterosexual), he said:

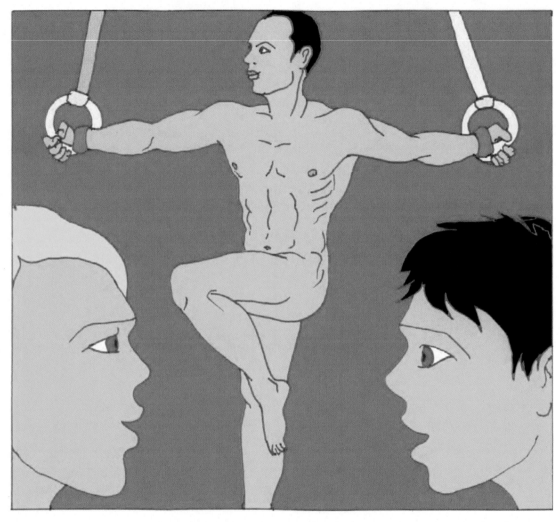

"I hope one day to live in a world where your sexuality is as irrelevant as whether or not you are right- or left-handed. We can achieve this by making coming-out a normal process, by doing things like I did—by coming out publicly, by talking about it publicly, helping people to understand" (October 25, 2020).

John: YES!!!

In making this graphic book
Wikipedia was a most useful source of information.
Roberto Gonzalez Fernandes's book,
Journeys (GMP: London, 1988) inspired it,
and Daniel A. Helminiak's book
What the Bible Really Says about Homosexuality
(Alamo Square Press, 1994) justified it.
Many, many thanks to Kittredge Cherry
and John Mabry of Apocryphile Press for their help
in producing a beautiful version of my graphic book.

Made in the USA
Middletown, DE
16 May 2022

65727502R40060